Also by John Binder

Before First Light (Poems)

New West

ALA Carte

Love
has its
Limits

Poems
by
John Binder

f/stop books

310 471-6317   f.stop.books@gmail.com

Contents

Love in Retrospect

Love lives on
in memory

much as it does
in fantasy

Time perfects
the good affairs

on the bad ones
it takes revenge

Make Me An Angel

He had watched her
from a distance
He felt he knew her
the way she moved
the way she smiled
the way she pretended
not to be aware.

She didn't need
to study him much
She felt his gaze
as if it were
his warm breath
on her bare skin
and it was heavenly.

Neither understood
nor questioned the magic
when finally, they met
and were thoroughly
thrillingly enchanted.

The first time
they were intimate
got naked together
to do what people do
it was supernatural.

They were transported
they floated away
out of this world
for light years
or so it seemed.

When they returned
he said to her
"God, you're an angel"
She blinked her eyes
and asked, astonished,
"Where in hell did
you come from?"

So, ever after that
when she wanted
to visit heaven again
she'd slink up close
she'd take his hand
she'd touch his cheek
she'd look up at him
starlight in her eyes
voice soft as a feather
"Do me a favor, please."

This was their ritual
sacred as a prayer
in a country church.
"What do you want?"
his innocent reply.

She'd whisper to him
as if she were begging
and granting a wish
"Make me an angel."

When she said that
he knew what to do
and she did too.
So they would go
bodies entwined
mouths together
off to heaven again.

The Carrot Or The Stick

In scary times like these,
said the wily rabbit,
I prefer the carrot
to the stick.

You can whip somebody
with that darn stick,
but I can eat this carrot
and hip hop away lickety split.

You can chase me if you want
Down the road, round the bend
across the field to my rabbit den.
But take care, whatever you do.

You know what a rabbit
like me could do
down in the briar patch
with a bunny like you.

She Came By To Say Hi

When she came over
to talk to him,
she didn't know
she'd stay for life.
He offered her dinner,
a glass of wine,
then he asked her
to stay for the night.
They did what folks
do in a bed together,
then they hung out
for a day or two.
They took in a movie,
went to a bar,
staggered home
fell into bed again.
Between sleepin' and boppin'
they talked and laughed
and talked some more.
Some of it serious,
all of it fun.
They little noticed
that love had begun.

They went to the store
to buy their food,
held hands as they
walked down the street.
He fixed her car,
she bought him clothes,
they even went to the dentist
hand in hand.
They went out of their
minds with joy,
when they were told
she was having a boy.

They nearly died
of shock when it aborted.
That pain subsided
but it never leaves,
and having shared it,
neither will she.

They didn't know
she'd stay for life,
to share their joy
and endure their strife,
when she came over
to talk to him.

Save The World

Here's how we restore
the ordinary virtues
we've lost along the way:
I help you, you help me.
We both help the stranger
whoever he may be.

Guide a blind man
across the street.
Adopt an orphan.
Rescue a dog.
Little things still
mean a lot.

Feed your soul
until it is strong.
Exercise compassion,
until we are all united,
'til all are loving
and once again kind.

Make love mean more
than just a thrill.
Cherish your friends.
Seek until you find
your soul mate
to love beyond pleasure.
Stop loving hate.

Summer Girl

She was the first
of the summer girls
to burst into bloom
with the glory of
new womanhood.
She dazzled us like
the first sunrise
we'd ever seen.
No exaggeration.
She'd been 'til then
a tall tom boy
a lithe athlete
to run jump swim
with the best
of any of us.
Her femininity
had new form now,
astonishing curves and
graceful undulations.
Where she
used to be pretty
she was stunning.

The boys who had
ruled the mountains
and the lake
until this moment
all marveled at
the warrior princess
who had invaded

our domain,
rendering us each
defenseless
at first glance.
When I beheld
this new vision
I was in a game
of touch football
with those boys,
the musketeers,
they'd called us
since we were kids.
We were almost men.
We had the bullets
and the guns
just no one
to shoot at,
not marksmen yet.
I caught a pass
downfield
then tumbled
head over heels.
The first glimpse
I caught of
our brand new woman
I was upside down.
The world was too.
I rolled over
sat up and just
stared at her,
in pristine tee shirt
pale shorts
issuing miles of legs.

She walked or strode
knowingly innocent
aware the world
was watching her,
and it would be
staring from now on.

Some time after that
we swam across the lake
the two of us
to a deserted
old wooden dock
with a ladder
up the front.
We took turns
diving in
the crystal water
doing flips
and twists
showing off
having fun
utter joy of life
bursting from us.
The thrill beyond
any I'd had before
was climbing up
that ladder first
then turning
to watch her
ascend like an angel
the rungs to heaven
ever so slowly
gleaming wet,

each time pausing
for a definite beat
when the water
weighed her top down
exposing her
brand new breasts
for my delight.

Up on the deck
she'd pull the straps up
recovering
and smiling at me
as her fingers
swept the water
from her hair
to make it run
down her shoulders
and the rest of her
as I would dream
of doing for days
nights and even
years to come.

We got together
once, years later.
Sad to report
it was fraught
and disappointing.
We were drinking,
she more than me.

It seemed unfair.
Her parents were
due to return.

I wanted to escape
and not destroy
the glimpse I'd had
of her perfection.

But the virtue
of memory and
its punishment too,
is that so little
of its essence
can be forgotten.

AI (Artificial Ignorance)

Is all hope gone?

Is the distance between
savagery and salvation
too great to traverse
on foot, or in a rocket
even, supersonically?

It always had been
nearly insurmountable,
the distance between
God's heaven and our earth.

He forgave our ignorance
until we consumed
the forbidden fruit

of the tree of knowledge
of good and evil,
or so they say.

But now our ignorant
innocence has given sway
to the knowledge of
our damned technology.

Earth is furious
at that transgression,
so, God won't
hear our prayers or
take our iPhone calls.

We thought we were
such ingenious beasts
trashing Sacred Earth
with infernal machines
of glory and destruction.

Is all hope gone?

Have we even got
the slightest prayer,
now that intelligence
is artificial and the ones
employing it are so
obliviously lethal?

Dog Tired In Houndsville
(A working man's lament)

"Dogs don't eat corn puddin",
she said,
"they don't eat coleslaw,
either, but somebody did."
She pointed at me.

Of course, it was me
but I'm in
one of my "moods"
as she puts it.
I feel ornery
as a sore tooth.

I say it louder,
"Must'a been one 'a
them kids for certain
made that puddin
and that slaw
disappear."

Truth is,
I don't know how she
puts up with me.
I used to be
a better fella
a steady nicer guy.
I went to work
and did a good job.

I drank a bit
but not completely,
and I only fought
when someone shoved me.

Then, without thinking,
I come to figure out
that I was standing still
and the world was
running away from me
faster than a rabbit
from a hound.

I should'a studied more
in school
and not gone fishin'
or shooting
every other day.
Now, everything is
digits and numbers,
not a hammer
or a wrench in sight.
It's all a big fuckin'
mystery to me.

I still love my wife
and my kids --
much as I can reach 'em
with them irritatin'
gizmos in their hands.

"Yeah, I ate the goddamn
corn puddin'
and I ate the damn slaw.

I washed it down
with whiskey and a beer
and I figure to have
at least one more."

I know I talk tough
and I won't admit
that I'm scared.

The world is
runnin' away from me
and I don't know
how to catch up.

Someday My Screwball Will Come

(for Jeanne)

When your mind is on fire
and the fibers of your body
vibrate with unfathomable fear
that you might just explode
or could virtually disappear
and no one would notice or care,
you can meditate, masturbate,
regurgitate all the platitudes
that the gurus and the cuckoos
have fed you over the years,
but nothing will help you like
that sudden thrilling encounter
with another screwball like you,
for whom you can fall and kiss
and ball and laugh yourself
silly all night and all day too,
and even if you fall to fighting
and fight 'til you're falling down
and rolling around on the ground,
it really doesn't matter because
fighting, laughing, crying,
kissing and balling is O.K.
if she or he is really truly is
a screwball like you.

Love Has Its Limits

The moment I saw you
I could hardly breathe.
You smiled and I felt weak.
You said hello
and I couldn't speak.
We danced and floated
like clouds in the sky.
You said you liked me,
I thought I would die.
We dated, we dined,
we talked for hours,
and when we fell silent
our beating hearts
were the loudest
sound in the room.

We touched, we kissed.
we made love
like we invented it.

Our passion remained
at a fever pitch
for quite a long time.

But the truth is,
a fever either kills
or a fever breaks.
Sad to say that
ours exploded
like a bomb.

The highest mountain
has a peak.
The deepest ocean,
has a floor.
No matter how it starts,
or how it feels,
love has enemies galore.
They lurk inside us.
They are all around us
and when we weaken
they sink their daggers in.

Love is glorious.
Love is grand,
Love can be infinite,
but we are proof,
my darling dear,
that love has its limits.

Flying Toward Sorrow

She is flying today
toward sadness
thousands of miles to someone
very close to her heart,
someone who is dying.
God go with her
perform a miracle
if you can.
Save the life
that is drifting away,
but if you can't or won't
because that is the way
you or fate has made it,
protect the one I love.
Let this sorrow
strengthen and instruct her
but bring her back to me.

The Endless Screenplay

I've been working endlessly it seems
on a screenplay, which, I can't
for the life of me, turn in the direction
of success, so I think I'll take a break
to discuss writing for the silver screen,
(or whatever little pocket device
people watch movies on these days).

The way movie drama works is,
someone wants something badly,
someone else opposes that dream.
The first someone often gets it,
then the second takes it away.
Sometimes it's a lot of money,
sometimes it's a beautiful girl
or a handsome muscle-bound guy.
Before we know it, the fight is on.
It's violent and bloody as hell,
knives and guns, bullets and bombs,
broken limbs and battered skulls,
whatever your mayhem requires.

In the end, the guy who wanted it,
usually gets it, whatever it was,
and the guy who fought him for it,
invariably gets a bullet in the head.

The winner is the good guy
and the loser is the bad guy,
though it's hard to tell them apart,

after all the wretched violence,
without that bullet in the head.

My impossible-to-finish screenplay
has no guns, bullets or bad guys.
There's a good woman, a nice man
and a pile of money involved.
The money is the object of desire,
until, of course, they fall in love.
It's charming and kind of funny,
but I can't seem to bring it home.

Then again, if I had no conscience,
like most who write for the screen
these days, I could solve it easily
by putting a bullet in somebody's head.
Sadly, in this case, it may be my own.

The End Is Nigh

Oh how we used to laugh
at those old cartoons
that showed a scrawny guy
with a beard and shaggy hair
carrying a sign that read,
"Prepare to meet your maker"
or "Repent, the end is nigh."
The backwards-yearning folks
in church, mosque and temple,
who dote upon the rants
that mad desert poets uttered
thousands of years ago,
took up the desperate chant,

"these are the end days,
repent, repent, repent.
It's (almost) all over now,
baby blue, Armageddon is just
around the corner from you."

All we good sinners know
that crooked preachers preach
to fleece us of our money.
So, we laughed and made fun.
and enjoyed our sinful ways,
until the weather changed.
Now fires rage, floods flow,
and these horrifying wars
come one upon another.

Is this the end of our world,
or just a period of change?
Mankind has adapted before.
This time we aren't so sure.
Now the crazy old man
in sackcloth and sandals
carrying that sign,
ain't so funny anymore.

*

The Traditional Hopi People,
whose time in this hemisphere
outdates the Bible and Koran,
have a scripture they live by.
It's not written on paper,
but inscribed on their souls.

It's called the Hopi Prophesy.
Traditional Hopi, like Tibetans
and some other ancient tribes,
feel responsible for the lands
that sustain them, our land, too.

Their most sacred spot of all
is the Black Mesa in New Mexico.
It is a mountain made of coal.
The ancient Hopi Prophesy
warns that if precious things
are dug from the earth,
as we mine Black Mesa Coal
the world may wither and die.

Our science and common sense
echo what the Hopi prophets knew,
what even that ragged old man
in the cartoons knew:
As the world heats and the ice melts
ancient truth and today's news
agree that the end indeed is nigh,
we must mend our ways or die.

Why Can't We

Why can't we
just be
human beings
all of us together
all of us the same
different shapes
and sizes
different color skin
different names
I belong to nothing
I belong to you
I don't believe
in a heaven above
or a hell below
I believe in love
bees in a hive
flowers in a field
cows in the barn
waves in the sea

Let's just be
what we are
I am you
and you are me
with just a bit
of space in between

Tom Paine's Revolution

The King asked the Queen
how he looked in his crown.
She said, "Powerful".

The Queen asked the King
how she looked in her gown.
He said, "Beautiful".

Neither asked if the King's power
and the queen's beauty
might possibly be temporary.

The People were hungry.
The People were angry.
They were starting to rebel.

The General rode
at the head of his army
on a prancing horse.

He had orders to conquer
to seize or to slay
any who got in his way.

But when the people rise
as one, no man on a horse
can beat them down.

The People are patient
through thick and thin
until a Revolution begins.

Then hell breaks lose,
chaos and war reign.
The beginning is the end.

Soon the ones on top
are on the bottom.
"The world is upside down."

In a world ordered properly,
as Mr. Paine instructed us,
the People wear the crown.

"We have it in our power to
begin the world over again",
and so we must once more.

But let us revolutionize
the world this time
without all the blood and gore.

The Imperfect Couple

She was gorgeously neurotic.
He was foolishly romantic.
It's hard to say which
was the bigger malady?

They could have been
the perfect couple,
She felt neglected.
He felt abandoned.

Her husband was cold.
His wife, preoccupied
with things she loved
more than she loved him.

It was a feverish fantasy,
Folie a deux, the French call it,
a "shared delusion"
their secret love affair.

They had clandestine meetings
in unlikely places
where sex if not quite love
carried them away.

It was electric and transcendent,
until her neuroses
and his conscience
simultaneously began to stir.

She promised one day to do
whatever he asked her to,
"Just don't ever ask me to
make up my own mind."

He found that disquieting,
Later, she called him
from a department store
in a dreadful panic.

She couldn't remember
how to get home, she said.
He came to her rescue
but he worried after that.

Her crazy started clouding
his romantic fantasy.
He looked into his wife's eyes
and saw suspicion there.

Yet the romance continued,
maybe better than before.
The riskier love is
the sexier it can be.

Desperation can make
true allies in war
and in love, temporarily,
but desperation
is a poor foundation
for a lasting dream.

Their pitiful bond
could not quite hold.
When it exploded
like a roadside bomb
it blew everything away.

Clandestine love
may be a rocket ride,
a supercharged thrill,
but top-secret lovers
should know such love
has the power to kill.

The Year The Bad Guys Won

Sometimes things
just go wrong
the car blows up
the barn burns down
the dog dies
it doesn't rain
it tests positive
love runs away
the bad guys win.
What can we do
but grab a bottle
find a lover
turn the music up
loud as it goes
party on down
knock ourselves out

let the world turn
on its own
as it often does
until the bottom
is back on top again
But if it does not
we'll sober up
make a new plan
and come back
harder next time.

They call that
revolution
It might be fun
Can we make a revolution
without a gun?

The Revolution Begins

A rich man passed a poor man
on the street who hissed,
"Come back here, Slick."

The rich man stopped, turned.
"Look me in the eye".
The poor man commanded.

The rich man took the dare.
He didn't get rich by
being shy or being scared.

"Where'd you steal your money?"
the poor man demanded.
"How do you know I'm rich?"
the rich man countered.

"'Cause you smell like money".
The poor man said with glee.
"And you smell like shit",
was the rich man's quick reply.

The poor man cackled sharply.
"Give me some money, rich man."
"And why would I do that?"
the rich man calmly asked,

"Because, I have this".
the poor man said,
as he pulled out a knife
and brandished it.

The rich man made a face,
and shook his head slowly,
reaching, as if for a wallet,
but producing a gun instead.

The beggar was shocked,
the rich man triumphant.
"You bring a knife to a gunfight?
No wonder you are dressed in rags."

The humiliated beggar slumped
and hung his head in shame.
A thousand times he'd lost,
and now he'd lost again.

The rich man sneered and tossed
some bills at the poor man's feet.
He tucked his gun away,
and strolled on down the street.

As he bent to pick up the money
the poor man knew it was enough
to get him what he really wanted,
and what he wanted now was a gun.

The Kindness Of A Stranger

I lived with a woman
in a little place
at the beach,
that was built up on
pylons or stilts,
looking out on the sea.

The waves rolled in
under the house
soothing our days
and at night
lulling us to sleep.
Kids and dogs romped
on the sand.
Surfers danced
down the waves.

Living there was
to live in heaven,
but cheap as hell.

This was before the rich
had bought up the beach
and pushed out
the surfers and
the real folks
for whom Poseidon
and all the gods of nature
had intended it.

I loved or I had loved
the woman
I was living with
in fits of passion,
that now were
turning into hate.
It doesn't matter why.
Loves thrive. Loves die.

She went off one day
to be alone, she said,
but maybe, I thought -
and maybe I hoped -
she meant to pounce
on another man
as she had
pounced on me.
If I sound bitter
it's because I believe,
foolishly perhaps,
that love should be
voluntary and it should
stay that way
or it should end.

I had tried
to leave her repeatedly
but she had resources.
I was weak
and she held on tight.
She was
harder to quit than
alcohol or cigarettes.

I took a long run
on the beach
one day,
when she was gone,
then a cooling plunge
in the sea.
I was loving my freedom
even if it was temporary.
As I came out of the water,
I smiled at a girl,

who smiled sweetly
back at me.
Her smile lingered
and that was all it took
to remind me that
as hard as love may
sometimes be,
sex often can be free.

We sat together
on the sand,
this sweetly smiling
woman and me.
We talked and laughed.
I didn't catch her name,
and she didn't even
ask for mine.

Her cottage was nearby,
We walked there,
shared a joint
in her 'crib',

as they used to say,
and together we rocked
our aloneness away.

If I were given
to philosophy,
I would postulate,
"The whole world
should be a sandy beach
where girls aren't afraid,
to smile back at you,
talk, laugh and get high,
then go off and screw".

Of course, real life is
full of "agro",
which is surfer-speak
for aggravation.
My girlfriend returned,
alas, from her vacation.

She burst in the door
with a gleam in her eye
that sent a shudder
down my spineless spine.
Her little trip away
had super-charged
her amorous battery.

Nothing I dread more,
sometimes,
than a woman
too revved up
with romantic energy.

She didn't explain
her transformation
and I offered no hint
of my sexual vacation.

Later, I took her to dinner
at a place down the beach
that we hadn't been to
in a while.
I was plotting
how to say goodbye.

As I studied the menu,
a soft voice welcomed us.
I'd heard the voice before.
I looked up to see the face
and the woman I had recently
been favored to explore.

I've had a shotgun in my face,
been punched in the mouth,
chased by rednecks down South,
beaten by a gang of jocks,
shot with a teargas grenade.
I've rolled a couple cars.
This moment chilled me more.

But our waitress betrayed
nothing as she greeted us.
She smiled at my girlfriend,
then smiled at me, evenly.
Not a hint of recognition.

I relaxed completely,
and gloated perversely.
I have enjoyed few meals
as much as that one.
It was consumed guilt free.

My girlfriend babbled
how bright our future
was bound to shine.
I had no idea nor a care
what had fanned her flame.
Perhaps it was precisely
what had invigorated mine.

I sipped my wine
and savored the memory
served up freshly
by the pretty waitress.

My happy companion
could not hear
the chains snapping
from around my chest.
She hadn't a clue
that this would be
our last meal together
and our final night
sharing a bed.

She bubbled and beamed
anticipating the thrill
we'd have making love

with the doors wide open
to the sound and the rhythm
of the waves rolling in.

I resolved to give her
at least that satisfaction
before announcing
in the morning
that I was gone.

A final sip of wine.
I signaled the waitress.
She smiled politely again.
I discretely smiled back
and thanked her
for the check
and silently for
so much more.

I must admit I do admire
a woman or a man,
for that matter, who knows
how to give and how
to accept so intimate a gift,
then simply says "so long".
I had a final night of love
with the woman
I had been living with.

In the morning I was gone.

Agnus Dei
Lamb (Chop) Of God

Did I create God?
Or did God create me?
How many angels can dance
on the head of a pin?

Do they sing
as well as dance?
or do they just
giggle and prance?

Do they do
the Macarena?
Do they show
a bit of skin?

As I walk upon the water
or turn water into wine,
these are the thoughts
that occupy my mind.

But most perplexing
are the questions
we've all been asking
since the dawn of time.

Does anything
that we believe
have any affect
whatsoever on reality?

if I believe in God.
does God believe in me?
Will I ever get a glimpse
of a dancing angel's knee?

Emotion Is Just An Illusion

They've taken away my emotions.
I feel them but we are estranged.
What was sadness is now depression.
An erotic urge is sexual aggression.
Life's thrills make me ecstatic.
but the joy I feel, I must conceal,
or they will pronounce me manic.
I forget a name, like any old-timer,
I will be labeled Mr. Al Zheimer.
The same with a flair of temper.
If I get angry, it's called distemper.
Mixed feelings are chronic confusion.
Should I lose interest, I've got ADD.
When I'm tired, I'm not weary, it's STE.
Poets made melancholy warm and soft
Now they destroy it with Zoloft.
Worry about something, it's paranoia.
Trust, as you can imagine, is naivete'.
Disgust, thankfully, is still disgust. Hatred
still remains in the game.
Jealously, rage and pain are the same.
And that, at least, makes me happy.
Or has happiness got a new name.

My Valentine
(to Jeanne)

Hand and glove
Wave and shore
Tom and Jerry
Butter and Jelly
Your foot and
the glass slipper
You and I are
the perfect fit.

Doggerel

Dogs don't care if you're uncool
Dogs don't care if you're a fool
Dogs don't care if you're a bum
Dogs just wish that you'd come home.

Dogs don't care if you're good or evil.
Hitler had a dog, so does the devil.
The devil's dog is called Cerberus.
He has three heads which all bite
and he guards the gates of hell.
If God has a dog, it's a shepherd
to herd his flock and guard them well.

Dogs don't care if you're rich or poor
Dogs don't care if you're ugly or pretty

Dogs don't care if you're dull or witty
Dogs don't care if you're white or black

Dogs just need a hug and a scratch
to love you wildly and have your back.

So remember this when you feel blue,
there's a dog out there just for you.

Love Is God

He could see it in her eyes.
She needed some attention.
She could feel in her bones
that he needed some love.

She had had none for a while.
He'd had nothing but grief.
On and on that went for them,
like it would never ever end.

It was wrong to even consider
that they might get together.
They were not deceitful people.
Each belonged to someone else.

Neither did much praying, but
Christ, how much loneliness
can two lonely hearts take?

Before You Were Gone

It was a gorgeous sparkling day.
We drove up the coast to Richard's
down the little drive and parked
under the tall eucalyptus trees
that some enterprising fool imported
from Australia years and years ago.
Don't ask me why. They grow fast,
somebody said, but so do children,
so does love, and sadness sometimes
can shoot up like a wicked weed
through the very smallest crack
in your heart, even if you thought
that happiness will last forever.
There was omen when we arrived.
Just as we stepped from the car
the earth shook, an earthquake.
A small one, we thought little of it.

It was a loud and happy party
full of people who were certain
we would all succeed at whatever
it was that we had come here to do.
Some of us were already on our way.
Some were on the verge of being stars.

We sipped and we sang, we danced
and flirted with each other's mates.
Not I, though, for once in my life
because I had you, and you had
brought me back from the edge

of the world, the brink of the cliff,
as I was tempted to take the plunge.

And you, I had opened as the sun
opens a flower, and I was proud.

We swam in the cold delicious sea,
lolled on the pillow-soft sand,
laughed like the world was a joke
that only the two of us were in on.

But parties do end, the lights come on,
there are bottles, glasses, dirty dishes,
left-over food, fag-end joints and cigs
in the ashtrays, all the detritus
that reality leaves us humans with
when we discover that ours was just
another party on a lovely afternoon
at Richard's cottage on the beach.

Long-lasting love was out of reach.

America's True History

Emmett Till was a black boy
from Chicago, just fourteen.
A white woman said
that he had molested her
as she tended to her store.
Then she said he whistled
at her as he went out the door.

Later, the woman's husband
and his brother-in-law
snatched up poor Emmett
took him to the woods
and beat him horribly
until his face was gone.
They shot him in the head
then they threw him
into the Tallahatchie river
tied to a heavy iron fan
they had made him carry
to the spot of his murder.

Days later he was found.
His family held a viewing
in his hometown Chicago
with the casket open
to show his mutilation
to the whole wide world,
to get revenge on the Ku Klux
bastards who had murdered him.

Thousands came to witness
what had been done to him.

The horror took place in 1958
in good ol' Mississippi,
home of bitter hateful men
who hadn't done enough
in centuries of slavery
to punish black Africans
for tending their crops,
scrubbing their floors
and raising their kids.

A white jury did not convict
the murderers, who bragged
to other loving confederates
how they had killed the boy.

The sickest part of the story
is that a few years ago
the white woman admitted
to somebody writing a book,
she made up the whole thing.
Poor Emmett Till did nothing
to threaten or to offend her.
But she never explained why
she did this horrid fabrication.

People are wonderful, I think,
except when we are the worst
creatures on God's green earth.
And still there are white folks
who hate black boys like poor

young innocent Emmett Till,
just because his skin was dark,
but it was not near as black
as those white folks' souls.

The Miserable Mystery Writer

He held the pistol in his hand.
felt the weight of it,
the way it fit his grip.
He was forced to admire it
handsome in a cold steel way
someone had designed it,
crafted it with love and irony,
when its purpose was to kill.

He was in no big hurry,
time to have these thoughts.
He was a mystery writer after all,
with no more mysteries to explore.

He raised the gun slowly
touched the muzzle to his head,
moment of truth, as they say.

What surprised him then,
having lived his life in fear,
he was not afraid to die.

This courage gave him pause.
It stilled his hand completely.
Why be afraid then and not now?

He tried to squeeze the trigger
but the effort was in vain,
hand frozen, his mind whirled.

Then it came to rest
on this solitary thought -
if death doesn't scare us,
it must be life that does.
How in the world can that be?

That mystery intrigued him,
and mysteries must be solved.
He slowly laid the pistol down
and quickly picked up his pen

Old Time Love Song

Lover boy, where have you been?
I have just been traveling.

Lover boy, where did you go?
I've been wandering high and low.

Oh, Lover boy, what did you do?
I promise you, I have been true.

But Lover boy, I missed you so.
From time to time I have to go.

Lover boy, can't you settle down.
There's a big world beyond this town.

Lover boy, I'm through with you.
You must do what you must do.

But, Lover boy, I still love you.
Yes, my darling I know you do,

But not as much as I love you.
Then, Lover boy, why not marry me?

I will if it will set us free.
How can marriage set us free?

Ours could have magic chemistry,
I become you and you become me.

Lie down with me and we shall see.

Men Also Cry

A man sat weeping
tears down his face.
He did not hide them
or wipe them away.
He just kept staring
out the window,
a mug of coffee
cold before him.
He was a young man
not yet middle age.

A woman noticed him,
an older woman.
She was surprised
to see a man alone
weeping so openly
without apology.

She wondered why.
He glanced at her.
She did not smile.
They shared the moment
but sadness itself,
when it runs so deep,
is impossible to share.

She would never know
the love he'd lost.
He could not imagine
her life of tears.

Time will teach him
what she can't say.
Everything we cherish
will be taken away.

True Adventure

The biggest thrill
of human contact
is the chance
to undertake
the dazzling search
for the character
mysteriously hidden
inside the person
whom I clearly see
standing right
in front of me.

We are each
a dark star,
an unknown planet
a jungle thicket,
which may require
a perilous expedition
through rugged terrain
to catch a glimpse
of the elusive soul
we are longing for.

Love is the conveyance
that can take us each
into the heart
of another's darkness
until we see the light.
It may not be a lover
who intrigues us.
It may be our child,
a parent, a friend
or a total stranger,
who is terrified
of discovery
and revelation.

If we are lucky,
sufficiently intrepid,
we may find
a pot of gold,
the Lost Ark,
a human treasure,
hidden there.

You better beware,
there are those
who shall remain
a mystery forever.
They may enchant us
like the jungle deep,
then entrap us there,
on the adventure
from which
we never return.

Just A Taste

I watched a humming bird
this morning.

Such a gorgeous creature,
flying, flitting, hovering
with impossible agility
and lightening grace,
sampling the sweetness
from the tempting buds
of the flowering trees
beyond the deck
on my hill.

She was the essence
of deft curiosity, but
not the settling kind.
I stood stock still.
She came near
and let me hear
the subtle sound
of her eponymous wings,
a whisper in my ear.

She looked me over,
then flew away,
but not satisfied with that,
she came back again
to look directly
into my eyes,
just as you did,
the first time you
looked me over and left,

then came back
for a second glance.

She reminded me of you
coming by for a touch
and a taste.
I guess it was obvious
I wanted to devour you,
so you flew away.

More buds, more flowers,
more sweetness everywhere.

That's why you
and that hummingbird
both have wings.

I Like To Get High

(song)

You know how it is
The world goes around
One day you are up
Next day you're down

You meet a girl
You make a date
You fall in love
It turns to hate

Tears fall like rain
pour down and splatter
Nothing you can do
to make it better

Say, I've had a bad day
I need a good night
I want to make love
She wants to fight

I try to be nice,
She thinks I am cruel
She gets all hot
I try to stay cool

I want to disarm her
with a kiss and a smile
But It's easy to see
that I've missed by a mile

She kicks me around
She curses my name
When I protest
she says I'm to blame

She makes me feel low
So low I could die
And when I'm that low...
I've got to get high.

Soon I am mellow
She doesn't like that
I tell her my pipe dreams
She says I talk through my hat

I try a new tack
a brand new direction
the one that should lead ~~to~~
to love and affection

I kiss her and touch her
I whisper sweet nothings
but the things that I tell her
she finds disgusting

That makes me feel low
so low I could die
And when I feel low
I've just gotta get high

Went dancing last night
Had a hell of a time
Downed a few drinks
And everything's fine

The music is swinging
The crowd is real swell
There's nothing like dancing
to make you feel...

Well...you know
how I really do
like to
get high!

Beautiful Poison

Friends tell me
to forget you
I'll surely rue
the day I met you

Beautiful poison
they say you are
A deadly blossom
black onyx star

But how can I help
the way that I feel?
I am powerless
in your velvet grip

Your laser eyes
your liquid hips
My fate is sealed
I am paralyzed

The lethal potion
on your lips
you let me drink my fill
a lovely way you kill

It is easy to see why
I'm not afraid to die

Beautiful poison
that's what you are
A deadly blossom
black onyx star

Shut Up

It was a perfect marriage.
Whatever he said,
she disagreed with.
Whatever she said,
he didn't even hear.
It was a brilliant harmony
often to be so far apart
but always staying near.
They had their ups and downs.
The downs never lasted long.
It was these fluctuations
that kept the marriage strong.
Smooth sailing gets boring
as she liked to say.
Truth is he wouldn't have it
any other way.
On this one thing
they did agree,
everything in life is costly
but love at least is free.

This Dream's For You

I wish that we each could have
the love that we all deserve.
Someone to touch and hold us
when the night is dark and long.
Someone to make us laugh.
Someone to keep us strong.
And wouldn't it be heavenly
to give the kind of love that
makes sad eyes sparkle again?
Touch their lips with yours.
Tell them a thrilling story.
Sing them a tender song.
It's sad to be so lonely.
It hurts to be so sad.
I wish we each could have
the love we so desire.
Anytime you need someone,
I hope someone will be there.

All Roads Lead To A Broken Heart

This love affair
was doomed from the start
All roads lead
to a broken heart

He first saw her
in the morning light
He first kissed her
on a magic night

When he touched her
the world stood still
He knew he loved her
and he always will

But love seldom goes
as we think it should
Love is a walk
in a deep dark wood

Some love affairs are
too good to last
like the tragic lovers
from the past

Romeo and Juliet
Bonnie and Clyde
perfect for a time
and then love died

This Love Affair
was doomed from the start
All roads lead
to a broken heart

The Gun & The Rope

Tired of being worn out
and sick of being poor,
he got himself a gun and
robbed the liquor store.
That first stick-up was easy,
so, then he robbed the bank.
Not a loser anymore,
an outlaw like Jesse and Frank.

With money in his pocket
he really went to town.
He got himself a woman
who laid her body down.
They drank and gambled
and raised holy hell.
It couldn't last forever.
but was heaven for a while.

Free as the west wind,
bad as Billy the Kid,
he did whatever he wanted
and loved whatever he did.
No more taking orders
or getting pushed around.

A couple fellas crossed him.
He shot those bad boys down.

The road to heaven is narrow.
The road to hell is wide.
His woman double-crossed him,
and then that woman died.

But the life of an outlaw
is not just endless fun.
He gunned that woman down
then he really had to run.

The chase was fast and furious.
He fled like a runaway train.
But it ended as it always does,
with him bound up in chains.

The judge asked him his reason
for behaving the way he had.
He told the judge, "Your honor,
I'm not proud of being bad, but...

I was tired of being all wore out,
sick of being broke and bored.
I just went and got a gun
and left judgment to the lord."

"That gun came with a rope, son.
to hang you with", the judge said.
"I can only judge the living.
I let the Lord judge the dead."

Beware, Jack

"Life is not fair", said the
handsome young man,
the golden boy, the unicorn,
whose life was blessed with
adoring family and friends,
with more money than
a hundred men could spend
and all the women
any man could want,
including the luminous beauty
he was married to.

He'd been a hero in the war,
risked his own enchanted life
to save the life of his friend.
He had success at everything.
Some of it was purchased
but a higher price was paid
after we made him President.

Eventually, the hateful men,
who do their evil in the dark,
or behind dark polished desks,
jealous of the young king,
who'd always had everything,
found a fool to take the fall,
when their hidden gunmen
put a bullet in the hero's throat
and another in his head.

As the world gasped and wept,
the villains, no doubt, laughed
and repeated what he once said,
"Right you were, young man,
life really is not fair."

Eternally Evil

The twin horrors,
immortal mortal sins,
of Indian genocide
and African slavery
still smother America,

a bloody animal hide
tossed over us, heavy,
hot and bloody wet
from the slaughter
house of our history.

They blanket us
with eternal guilt,
and still provide
inspiration for some

to hurl the hatred
of their ancestors
at those perceived
as "others" today
not really American.

They take aim at
immigrants,
at blacks,
at gays and such
at the damaged
at the poor,
at women, even.

And why?

Are past atrocities
so indelible,
so unforgivable
that their karma
will only burn
by the destruction
of us all?

Oh.
Weep for America.
What evil we have done.
What evil we still do.

LRRPs

At a party in Austin years ago at
my friend "Kit" Carson's house,
I met two young men who were
just back from Vietnam.
They were black guys, and
they were quiet among us whites.
We were all males, drinking.
Someone passed a joint.
I shared it with the G.I.'s.
I'd been in the Army
but not to Vietnam.
I had also spent a lot of time
marching and protesting and
making films against the war.
I had a keen interest in it,
as I hated the thought of it.

Soon enough we talked,
or one of the soldiers did.
The other one was silent.
He was either shy or damaged,
I could not really tell.
They were combat veterans
in the thick of the shit
in the jungle for a year

The one who did talk
told me things I'd heard
from others who'd been there
then he froze me cold.

I was in a LRRP squad",
he said, translating for me,
"Long Range Reconnaissance.
We're scouts. We go on patrol
beyond the perimeter and look
for what's coming to get us."
He paused a lot as he spoke,
memory taking its toll.

"We make it up to this ridge
and we can see a few of miles."
He paused as the image bloomed.
"Mostly it was jungle canopy, but
we could see sections of a trail,
and where there were breaks
in the trees we saw personnel,
trucks and equipment moving.
It was a fucking army, man,
and it was heading south."

He took a hit off a joint,
passed it to his silent friend,
and said "my buddies and I..."
His friend smiled, strangely,
at his memory of the moment.

"We turned and hauled ass,
ran for miles, back to the base.
Couldn't call a chopper in.
That would've given us away"
He took a long pause this time.
His friend got up and walked away.

"I went into the command tent,
told my old Captain what we saw.
He told me to go get some chow.
There was a table of food
at the back of the tent.
I went and chowed down."
He talked like a machine, now.
Just the facts came out.
"After I ate, I fell asleep,
right in the back of the tent."

The machine paused for a moment
then he went right on reporting.
"When I woke up", he said,
All the officers were in the tent.

The Colonel was talking.
'If it's a whole division or such,
like the kid says, we need time.
We have to slow that train down.
We won't be able to stop it,
until it gets here and we're ready
with tanks and all we've got.'

No pauses now to search for words.
The Long Range Reconnaissance scout
Remembered every dreadful detail.
"The Colonel looked at my Captain,
and he said, Cap'n Drake, it's you
and your company are gonna go
and slow those bastards down.
I'll send a couple more companies, too".

The scout went on to describe
how his Captain turned white,
or would have if he could have
for he was black like the kid
who was telling me this story.
"But Colonel, that means that
all my men will die, sure as hell."

The Colonel's eyes turned to stone
and he said, "Yes, Captain, you
and all your men will die."
Then silence in the tent for a time,
according to this young man
who was telling me the story.
He said he was hardly able to breathe,
but he made a sound and the others
in the tent realized he was there.
The Colonel turned to him,
as he sat there on the ground.

He said "Son, you stay right here
in this tent. You can't go back
to your outfit and tell anybody,
not your best friend, <u>nobody</u>,
that they are all going to die,
because if you tell them,
maybe they won't go, and then
every man on this base may die."
The young soldier looked hard at me. He
wanted me to feel a fraction
of what he had felt at that moment.

I tried hard not to look away.
As his eyes held mine, he cried,
but he did not so much as blink.
He wept with his eyes open wide.
"They were all my old friends.
Over there you get real close.
and I couldn't tell them that
they were all going to die."

Evolution Is No Solution

A Neanderthal named Ug.
met a man named Bob.
Ug was carrying a club.
Bob had a sleek gun.
Squinting past the language barrier,
they took the measure of each other.
They circled round as animals do.
Ug hunch-backed and bent-kneed,
Bob standing tall and straight.
Ug smiled and drooled a bit.
Bob recoiled at a whiff of shit.
This fella doesn't bathe, he figured,
his finger on the trigger.
When Ug pointed at Bob's gun,
obviously curious what it was,
Bob leveled it in his direction.
Ug wielded his weapon
and clubbed a rabbit hopping by.
Bob fired his rifle at the sky.

Ug's jaw dropped even further,
his drooling spittle now a flood.
Dreams of mayhem and murder
lit a candle in each clouded eye,
lusting for that stick of thunder.
Bob knew he had a choice to make.
Walk away or shoot this ugly guy.
Neanderthal may dream of power.
Modern man has it in his hand.
Evolution has improved our posture,
the way we walk, the way we stand.

But Ug and Bob are not so far apart.
Bob chose to put a bullet in Ug's heart.
Such is man's fate right from the start.

Duty Kills

I killed a child today,
maybe two or three.

I mined the fields,
where food is grown.

Last week, a hospital
and a school, I bombed.

There used to be a city
just over that hill.

The enemy burrowed in.
What else could I do?

The people ran away,
those with legs to run.

I hate bombing cities
they have artillery there.

A man could lose his life
doing things like this.

But I boldly carry on.
Duty is not voluntary.

I must do what I must do,
defending our economy.

Perhaps

Some things never end
they just begin again
Not only night and day
waves upon the shore
love becoming hate
peace that turns to war
peace breaks out again

Tomorrow becomes today
Everything repeats
like a song's refrain
echoing in a canyon
flowers after the rain
the light in your eyes

A breath becomes a sigh
touch after touch
delight after delight
grace that's born of sin
now if only you and I
could live and love again

Ecstasy

Have you ever lain
upon your back
atop a hill
stared straight up
at the starry sky?
A breeze whispers
the trees sigh
an owl questions
who you are
but you just laugh
and do not care.

Your heart expands
all the way to infinity.
There is nothing
it seems between
you and anything
else in the universe
A single molecule
and the moon
are the same.
God, whom I
never could picture,
can be felt
if not seen
in everything
and everything
is she or it or him.
Words fail
or don't apply.

The only word
for what you
feel and see,
indeed for
what you are,
is ecstasy.

Just Ask

If you have ever
had the pleasure
of training a horse
you will know
the basic rule
is always to ask,
simply and clearly
and not to demand.

A horse will gladly
do your bidding,
so long as he
can understand.
But if you push him
he will push back
against your hand.

Tap him lightly
with your heel,
he'll step aside.

Squeeze both heels,
he'll go right ahead.
Tighten the reins,
and he will yield.
Release,
and he will relax.
Whatever you want,
just ask.

He will comply
or he will try,
so long as he has not
been spoiled or abused.

If we understand
what is asked of us,
if we have not been
mistreated and confused,
if asked in a way
we understand,
we will try to comply.

But if you mistreat us,
then we tend
to kick and bite,
to bolt or fight,
like a horse
who only wanted to do
what he or she
was asked to do.

So, if we want the world
to do our bidding,
stop pushing and abusing,
stop bombing and killing.

Just ask.

Go To Hell

When I saw
those celestial eyes
they promised me heaven.

When you turned
and walked away,
I looked for wings.

I was so dazzled
I forgot to ask
your name.

I knew that I
would see you again,
if only in my dreams.

When we met once more,
you smiled, we talked.
My dream came true.

I was thrilled to learn
that heavenly creatures
do carnal things.

When you disrobed,
I could attest
there were no wings.
Nonetheless, we sailed
to heaven and basked there
for a while.

Then you smiled
upon another man,
you now prefer.

Oh, you are an angel,
but then again,
so was Lucifer.

A Lucky Man

I sometimes feel guilty
for my wonderful life.
I've got a good dog
and a fabulous wife.

We don't have much money
but we get by.
Don't get drunk anymore.
We don't even get high.

We play at our work
and laugh a lot.
Go to bed early,
like as not.
I do feel bad for folks
in much of the world
with not enough love
and too little food.

Our fortune in life
seems to depend
on luck and geography
or if God is your friend.

Maybe there's a reason
I've got it so good,
but damned if I know
any reason I should.

I've done my best,
but nothing that great.
I've tried to spread love,
and fight against hate.

The sun comes up
and the sun goes down.
Life's not fair,
and the world is round.

It's a gorgeous place
with every pleasure.
It's also a jagged rock
with very sharp edges.

Past

All those friends
gone
suddenly remembered,
glimpsed again
through the mist
of years.

My heart stops
when I remember
your smile.

I guess
we're supposed to cry
every once in a while.

Advice For Us Old Soldiers

Old age is like going to war.
You are on the battlefield,
constantly scanning the heights,
knowing you are or will be
soon in the enemies' sights.

Surrounded by allies and friends,
you are existentially alone.
Much as you fight to deny it,
terror is rooted in your bones.

The worst of it for most of us
is that constant nagging dread.
Asked how he lived in the shadow
of death, Che Guevara said,
"I live like I'm already dead."

I Am Blind

I don't see old age
I don't see color
I don't see limited
I don't see slow
I don't see not pretty
I don't see hate
I don't see pain

I don't see inequality
I only see love
I see beauty everywhere
I see it in everyone
I see it in everything
I am a new American
I live the American dream
I don't live in that
old America anymore
I am free
Come live with me

Don't We Love One Another?

I hear you ask the question,
"Is that a man over there
or just pile of clothes?
Oh, it moved, I think.
Is it someone sleeping
or trying to sleep out here
in this terrible weather?"

I am homeless and hungry,
I am cold and lonely.
My clothes are ragged.
I sleep where I can.

As people go by me
they eye me warily
to see if I'm dangerous,
but I am harmless
except maybe to myself.

I fought in two wars.
A bomb exploded near me.
It almost killed me.
I lost five friends.
I suffer from PTSD.
My nerves are jangled.
My mind gets confused.

I am scared.
I am in pain.
I am depressed.

I am nearly hopeless
but not completely,
for this is America.

We love one another.
We care for each other,
for the down and out,
for the wounded,
for people like me.

But, hey, if that is so,
how can all this be?
Why do all you people
just tiptoe past me?

Luck & Fortune

He came down from the hills
to pay a visit to his lover.
But while he was off hunting gold
she'd taken up with another.
Fortune isn't only measured in gold.
Luck doesn't run in just one direction.
If you leave your lover behind
when you head for the hills,
she might go fortune hunting, too.
If you are young enough and lucky
you never know what you may find.
But when you lose your looks
and you lose your lover

you may not find another.
If I ever go hunting gold
I'll take my treasure with me.
Up in the hills, the nights are cold
and I wouldn't want her to miss me.
Life is not all about money.
Love is better than gold.
Many things can go wrong
out in the wide wild world.
If things really go bad
and I'm going down for good
I want her there to kiss me.

My Rules Are For Me

I am not a desperado.
I am just a lonely man.
I've been to war
and I've been to sea.
I survive as best I can.
Your rules are for you.
My rules are just for me.
I wear a gun.
It's oiled and clean
I can use it expertly.
But I bear no malice
for anyone who means
no harm to me.

There's a woman I love,
who once loved me.
She married another
as I was out to sea.
I ride now to find her.
If she still wants me,
I'll take her from any man
who tries to keep her
against her heart's desire.
I am not a desperado.
I am just a lonely man.

We Are All Salmon

I recently watched
a nature documentary
that offered me
a surprising consolation.

The ultimate truth is
everything dies.
I mean everything
that lives dies.

Everything large,
everything small,
from the majestic,
to the infinitesimal.

Mammoths to microbes
redwoods or movie stars,
even the billion stars
in the sky will all die.

I admired the salmon,
swimming upstream
pitting their strength
against the rushing water
over rock and rill
with all their might
and all their will,
their destiny to fulfill.

Their Journey done,
the spawning fish
lay their eggs and die
as will you and will I.

Everything everywhere
that ever was
or ever will be
faces the same fate.

There is nothing to fear
If we are all brave salmon
just swimming upstream
to lay our eggs and die.

Who Can That Be

In these late innings
as my mind gets slow
and my memory goes,
my legs are weak
my back is sore,
my temper flares,
no one cares
what I have to say
because I have hair
growing out of my ears.

I wonder who, too,
that old man is
who keeps staring at me
from the mirror.

Old age adds perspective
they tell me.
Unfortunately, it's a bit
like looking out
on a stand of trees
after a forest fire,
getting a preview
of my cremation

Love's Illusions

A lady on a paint horse,
went dashing by
at a passionate pace
her long yellow hair
streaming in the wind
like a golden cloud
across the sky.
His heart went racing
wildly after her.
Quick as he could,
he saddled up and
rode off in pursuit.

He had to know her,
see her face,
look her in the eye,
he knew not why.
Was she real or was she
a phantom, a mirage?

He'd been out on the plain
so long, he might as well
have been on the moon.
In the Big Bend Country
illusion can replace
reality like a potent drug.
He had seen Indians
chasing buffalo thundering
silently across the sky.

Is it ghosts you see out there?
A reflection, a vision, a dream?
A cowboy or a cowgirl must know,
if they are inspired or insane?

He rode like lightening,
but like the lightening
he couldn't catch her.
He would know her
at a single glance.

Did anyone know her?
Had anyone seen her?
That paint horse she rode
was as unforgettable as she?

He searched in every town,
every tavern, boarding house
brothel and ranch, to no avail.
Few men would be so avid
to a lover, let alone
to a woman glimpsed by chance.

And then, he met an old lady
at a cabin on the plain
and he asked about her again.
She laughed loud
when he described her,
a flash of lightning
in the old hag's eyes.

"You can't know this lady,
you've just seen flashing by.
You cannot have her.
You cannot hold her,
even if you chase her
until the day you die."

"Who is she", he asked,
in utter desperation?
"She is all that I
have ever dreamed of."

The crone laughed again,
"That she is, indeed, and
she's all you'll ever dream.
That is where her beauty lies,
in your hot desire as much
as in the speed of her steed,
and the flash of her eyes."

The witch's own eyes narrowed.
"She is the apotheosis
of your soul's every need, son."
Her cackle was hideous as if
the devil himself was laughing.
"You know what that word means?"
He shook his head, he did not.

"It means everything we aspire to
whatever we lust after,
whatever we chase, is fleeting,
but you might possess that beauty
if you stop riding, chasing,
and just simply stand still."

He took the hag's advice and
eventually his dream did appear.
He was drinking in a saloon,
playing cards with friends.
when she came in the door.

He didn't move, he couldn't.
She didn't look at him
for the longest time,
but when she did, she smiled,
and never looked away again.

Why would a man chase a phantom
across the land with but a glance
to spur him, a glimmer of hope
to keep him riding day after day,
and night after night?

It's beauty we are chasing,
magic we are searching for,
but love is the treasure
at the end of the rainbow
and it cannot catch us
if we keep chasing it away.

You And I

You and I
and the rainbow
We are the pot of gold
Better than luck
this is love
We share one heart
one set of lungs
You breathe out
I breathe in

You and I
and the sunrise
see the world
through the same eyes
No such thing
as being alone
One plus one is one
I know it's forever

This heaven is eternal
I will always be
where you are
It's physical
and it's mystical
It's real as a dream
You and I
and the morning star

Plus Or Minus

My loss is your gain
Your joy is my pain
It hurts to say so, but
love is a zero-sum game

Sunlit mornings
Moonlit nights
I thought we enjoyed
even our fights

Positive to negative
So good to too bad
Immeasurably happy
to incalculably sad

What are we here for
if not for each other?
I thought I was born
to be your lover

But that's not
what the ledger shows
A beautiful start
but a terrible close

You've got a new interest
I'm gone
Just like that
you're moving on

My loss is your gain
Your joy is my pain
It hurts to say so,
my deductible darling, but
love is a zero-sum game

Beware The Snake Who Charms Us

Pity those with the twisted gene,
who hate love and love to hate.
Go ahead and love your enemies,
as Jesus said, if you can,
but do not hold them harmless.
Don't mistake the fierce beauty
of the rattlesnake, who charms us
for something you can touch
and take to your chest.
The viper's bite is deadly.
The human snake, deadlier still.
There is no antidote,
except to steer clear or to kill.

Spiritual Zero

The devil paid a visit
at four o'clock in the morning
to taunt me with my fears,
redouble all my doubts,
deflate all my ambition.

St. John of the Cross called it
"The Dark Night of the soul".
I call it, "Spiritual Zero"
a blackness you can feel
a bleakness as unnerving as
a corpse in a funeral shroud.
A few disturbing thoughts
become an existential dread.

Everyone has trials like this.
For some I know it's endless.
I don't presume to give advice
to other tortured souls.
I do know that if you run
from a tiger he'll chase you
and eat you if he can.
The beast thrives on terror.
This devil is just the same.

I had a longtime dream impending
with which I was obsessed.
I thought it might define me
as a failure or success.

A foolish thought, I know,
but fools do thrive on dreams.

As I tossed and turned
and worried over my ambition,
that illusion opened the door
that let the devil come in.
Behind him streamed my fears.

Everyone of them danced before me,
a line of hideous chorus girls.
My suffering became unbearable
and since I could not take it
I perversely chose to embrace it
like a shell-shocked soldier
walking unarmed into enemy fire.

Maybe fear is just resistance
to all that we cannot control.
I let myself enter and explore it.
It was a weird and haunting land
full of ghosts of myself
from early childhood to old age.

It became a fascinating delirium
a lifetime accumulation of fright,
painful as you can imagine,
then mysteriously it transformed
and became devoid of emotion.
I can almost say I enjoyed it.

All that was replaced, eventually,
by a profound state of calm.
My grand ambition hardly mattered.

Perhaps that calm is the dream
I had always been searching for.

What might work for you when
the devil comes I cannot say.
I will tell you this, though,
since you cannot run or hide,
when he is at your door
you can open it and let him in.
Serve him coffee if you like.
But when he's done, stand firm,
look him straight in the eye,
speak from your very soul
and tell him to go to hell.

Revenge Considered Cold

This in something
I should not admit,
but as truth is my
commander, I shall.
I just imagined killing
someone I hate.
It was not an exercise
in the abstract,
not make-believe,
but really for real,
someone I think
I have reason to kill.

I considered carefully
how I would do it
and if I would likely
be caught or not?
Would the satisfaction
make me not care?

We've seen so many
movies about murder.
They are about
the only kind we see.
But when you imagine
yourself doing it.
It's more interesting
than a film can be.
It's not an actor
on the screen,
it's me.

The reason I'm sure
that I was serious is
that I had no emotion.
My conscience was clear
and cold as ice.

I have thought about
killing before.
I was in the Army -
though never to war.
In bayonet drills
I stabbed a sand bag,
with every thrust
screaming "kill! kill!"

It makes you think
what a soldier will do.
Initial reluctance becomes
an ominous thrill.
There are various
guns you shoot
that make you also
feel that you can kill.

The thought of doing
violence this time
was not exciting but
a cold-blooded thing.
I was Raskolnikov
in "Crime And Punishment"
contemplating how to waste
a nasty old woman.
In my case, it was a
cunning old businessman
who would steal from me
all that he can.

Having weighed
the pros and cons of it,
the pleasure and consequence,
I decided I didn't want
the karma it would create.
It would hurt my
loved ones too much,
and now that I write this
I just don't dare.

But I'm glad I considered it,
almost proud to know
I could do it, if I wished.
It makes me more
of a man, I think,
than that sneaky old
son of a bitch
....or perhaps I'm just
more of a fool.

Growing Up In America

Since Daddy got off cocaine
the kids were doing fine.
Easier to deal with since he
swapped his drugs for wine.

Momma ran off with Jesus
or that's what people said.
The kids knew from childhood
she wasn't right in the head.

Obsessed with the apocalypse,
a word the kids couldn't spell,
Daddy said, for all he cared,
Jesus could toss her into hell.

Growing up in America
is hard to do these days.
The grownups are like children,
undeveloped in so many ways.

It's all anger and ignorance,
if it isn't drugs and booze.
Everybody hates everybody.
How can kids learn to love?

America had a dream once.
We had promises to keep.
How can our kids dream
if they can't even sleep?

There are miracles, of course,
and each new generation
brings a fresh wave of hope
to revive a dying nation.

Still, growing up in America
is hard to do these days.
Everything a kid sees seems
shattered in a thousand ways.

Dearest John

John Lennon died today.
About the saddest words
that one could say.

Not the Holocaust
or the apocalypse
but still a cosmic loss.

Each generation has its genius
that they all love best.
He awakened all of us.

He was all about love
not just music and song.
Among eagles, he was a dove.

But fiercely so.
"Give Peace A Chance",
the war cry of John and Yoko.

Another sacred poet said,
"Truth is beauty, beauty truth".
Well, both are gone, John is dead.

We wallow now in mediocrity,
artists and leaders peddling
ugliness and awful mendacity

When so many people love you,
there will be those who hate.
He knew what they might do .
Like Jesus, he would say,
"They're gonna crucify me".

Alas, John Lennon died today.

Daydreaming On A Plane

Looking out the airplane window
on the clouds,
seeing my soul out there
floating.
On it I see a record
of my deeds,
all my sins,
my virtuous gestures,
that record God will scan
at the gates of heaven
as the nuns assured us
to frighten us to virtue
scare us into eternity.
Why am I ashamed
of all I've done
and not done?
It's pitiful.

And why am I ashamed
even of that emotion?
But then I see,
or imagine that I see,
a banner emerging
from the nebula.
There is no God
I'm as sure
as one can be
of godlessness.
But there is all the glory
that was created,
is perpetually created.

And that is not a myth.
It is infinite
exquisite reality,
hope and pain and beauty.
I look again.
My soul is clean.
I am not ashamed.

Letter From The Devil

Dear Donny T,

When are you coming
down to see me?
The folks in hell
sure do miss you.
There's a bunch of
well-roasted women here
dying to kiss you.

Well, not dying,
they're dead already,
and they are here
because they're evil.
We both know
the evil-dead
are just your
kind of people.

I know the cops are
closing in on you
to make you
face the music.
But don't surrender.
Just get a gun
from one of your big
game-killing sons,
put it to your head.
and...well you know
what to do.

One thing about
the girls in hell,
given their condition.
You can do anything
you want with them.
You can hug them.
You can kiss them,
You can even grab
their lifeless pussy.

You'll be free of all
that fuss up there.
Come on down
as they say on
"The Price Is Right".
Down here the price is free.
I'll be here to greet you.
Hell is the one place
your cruel and crooked

ways are not an issue.
In fact, down here,
your sins are virtue.

Sincerely,
Your ol' pal,
Lucifer (aka Satan)

Help Me

I am homeless
a cry of anguish
spit it like a curse
say it as a prayer
homeless hopeless

On the corner
at the light
she stood
holding a sign
"Help me"
is all it said

Layers of clothing
drape her body
like shingles
on a roof

She sleeps
in the cold

in the rain
with no protection
from endless harm

The few dollars
I offer will bring
just moments' relief
enough for a sandwich
and a drink

She ambles over
She is small
her face damaged
front teeth missing
but when she smiles
oh god
what sweetness
and gratitude

I am astonished
at her generosity
She offers me
a precious glimpse
of her heart

I wish her luck
such pitiful irony
good luck indeed

I drive away
and find myself weeping
for the homeless
for the hopeless
for her

God forgive America

On The Banks Of The Delaware Again

On the banks of the river,
on the brink of defeat,
an impossible idea
inspired their Commander
to make a decision
a mad man might make.
Sometimes it takes
madness to save the day.
They crossed the freezing
river in the dead of night.
That had never been done
with an army before.

They attacked the sleeping
Germans at dawn,
who had spent the night -
it was Christmas eve -
drinking, carousing.
They could barely rouse
themselves to fight.
The victory was not
the birth of a nation,
just a pause
in a string of failures
but it planted the
seed of freedom
in the fetid desiccated
womb of tyranny.

Years of war would be
democracy's incubation.
Desperation can inspire
radical choices.
Crossing the river
was a desperate deed.
We are on the banks
of that river again.

We must trust
our boldest inspiration,
load horses, cannon -
all the gear of war –
and launch our boats
in the frigid night.

True courage
is too proud to surrender.
History tells us
victory is never assured.
Just know that
only the brave hearts win.

I Want

I want to be
wildly in love
with the world.
I want to soar
with abandon.
And if I plummet
I shall do it
spinning spiraling
doing summersaults
all the way down.

I want to go back
to the days
when I laughed
like a fool,
skipped like a child,
tipped my hat
to passing strangers,
sang at the top
of my lungs
for no other reason
than It felt
so goddamn
good to be
infinitely alive.

I want to run
through the woods
wade in a stream
lie on my back

in a grassy field
howl at the moon
gawk at the stars.

I want to live
in sympathetic
rhythm with
the rock 'n roll
beating heart
of the universe,
shake like a leaf
spin like a top
'till I'm dizzy.

I want to go
insanely craaaaazy
and never stop
until the day
I defiantly spit
in fate's eye
and very simply
gleefully die.

Hip Hop Ain't Be Bop

Things are going good
just the way they should
The cat is in the cradle
The soup is in the ladle
The weather's getting warm
It's doing a lot of harm
with negative potential
The rain it is torrential
The "ex" is gettin' "stential"
Ain't nothing I can do
but snuggle up to you
That'll make it hotter
Hearts'll melt like butter
but I won't try to fool ya
I wanna slip it in the cooler
Fee fi fo fum
whoa baby here we come
You may think I'm flirty
and this is getting dirty
but that's not true
I just get kinda horny
when I look at you
Things are going good
just like I said
Honey, you put the yeast
in our baked bread.
Now you and I can feast
until we're dead
Be bop be bop be bop ...

Deep Dark Despair

There ain't a lot of
justice in this world
None if you ain't white
Life is hard for some
Easy as pie for others
as long as they be rich
You can work for a living
You can steal to survive
Neither way is easy
You can carry a gun
You can lie with numbers
Some preach the bible
Some sell their bodies
Some do dope and die

Everybody dreams of heaven
One day it'll all be swell
Except for all the ones
doomed to live in hell
I feel sorry for them but
tell ya the truth about it
I'm too damn beat to care
lost in deep dark despair

The Filthy Rich

What shall we do
with the ultra rich?
I don't mean
the merely wealthy.
Some of them do work
for their money.

I'm talking about
the filthy rich
the ones with "b"
before their "illions",
which may very soon
be in the "t" rillions.

It would be fun
to lock them up,
but I don't suggest
we kill them.
If we did that
we'd never find out
where in the world
they stashed
our money.

They rule us all
like pirate kings,
their pirate ships
now luxury yachts
on the seas of glitter
that money brings.

It must be fun
to live that way,
but even if
you admire them
don't pretend
they're not a problem.

Karl - not Groucho -
Marx once said,
who controls
the means of production
controls the world,
or something like that.

From the sweat
of our collective brow,
they collect a giant
tax deduction.
Their stocks rise,
bank accounts swell,
They thrive on
our labor.

Any crumb
tossed our way
is a just a little favor.
You want a living wage,
health care, pre-school,
a college education?
Something's got to give.

They can't be
so very rich
if they let you
fully live.

They own
the government,
which they claim to hate
because of all
the taxes they avoid
and those pesky regulations.
I say, if it doesn't
serve them as they wish,
give it back to us...
before we rise up
and take it.

As Light Goes Dark

The secret agent trench coat,
the slouch hat and dark glasses,
should have given him a clue
that she was not to be trusted.
But he was quickly taken captive
when that trench coat parted
and a glimpse of her
naked legs arrested him.
He lost all caution after that.
He wanted her, he needed her,
and soon he was helpless
as a kitten in her arms.

It was blissful for a while
then she betrayed him
to enemies he didn't dream
that he could have -
suspicion, jealousy and guile.

How could he have known
that she was on a mission
to make filleted fish
out of men like him?
It was as if Mata Hari
set her sights
on a putz named Larry,
or the treacherous beauty,
Delilah, had put curlers
in Sampson's hair.

It is not fashionable now
to blame women for
men's weakness
but let's be honest, fair.
There will always be
a war between the sexes
and he was unprepared.
That war is fought in ways
complex and subtle,
but men bring a knife
to a machine gun fight,
as the saying goes,
or maybe it's most true,
that feminine beauty
is the atom bomb.

He did what he did
and he did it well.
She was enraptured
or pretended to be.
She focused all her heat
on him and he melted
like butter in a hot pan.

He told her his tales,
she told him hers.
His were true as such
yarns may be.
Hers were a storm
of dazzling fantasy.

She'd been everywhere,
She'd done everything.
It seemed impossible
for one so young.

She'd won the lottery
but lost the ticket.
She'd been good
and she'd been wicked.
She had been a hero
and a villain.
She saved a woman's life
and her child.
She confided that
she'd even killed a man.
He was shocked
to his shoe soles by that.
He made a note to stay
on her good side -
which was tricky, since
all her sides looked good.
"Why did you kill him?
Was he a monster?"
"He was OK", she said,
"until he annoyed me."

Later, in a quiet moment
he asked her,
"How did you kill
that guy you killed?"
"Which one?" she said,
making his head spin.
"Don't tell me you
killed more than one!"
Her eyes narrowed
to sharp knife edges.
"I'm not saying anything",
she said and she smiled.

He knew he was staring
at the devil's face.
How could such beauty
be so terrifying?
Smiling, beguiling,
she shed her clothes.
Some forces are
too great to fight.
He let the devil take
him to heaven.

You might guess
they didn't stay together
long after that,
but he did not run away.
She had him,
and he stayed with her,
until she simply
disappeared one day.
Not every love
affair is like that,
or maybe, down deep
inside, they are.
Two hearts can't
beat as one unless
they grow together
or one heart dies.

He thought about
the men she killed,
or the ones she said she did.
You may believe it or not,
but he liked to think

the worst of her.
It thrilled the wilder
side of him, the dark side
he never knew he had.
He was proud his lover
was a killer, too much
in love to kill him, apparently.

And so they had a very
fine time, until she
disappeared mysteriously.
Everyone wondered about
the beautiful girl who seemed
to be so much in love with him.
Some even looked at him
suspiciously, as they might,
because that dark side
had taken over him.
But when they asked of her
he shrugged and told them
"she was fun, she was OK".
However he did not say
"until she annoyed me."

This Used To Be America

I'm just standing here
waiting for a sandwich
and a cup of soup
Nothing on my mind
but hunger and pain
I'm so used to them
they hardly bother me
My arm is numb

I don't know why
Might be my heart
Maybe I'll die
I survived a war

I can take this
Would have thought
I'd have a house
when I came home
I did for a while
Had a wife too
But If a man
can't stay sober
what's a wife to do
I didn't kill
anybody in the war
or maybe I did
You can't always tell
One I could've shot
Had the drop on him
but he was just a kid
so I let him live

Still think about him
Wonder if he's
down and out like me
I love my country
or I used to
Not sure now
what America is
I thought this was
the promised land
Maybe what we did
to so many others
for centuries
is being done to us
I hope not but
I've gotta move
There's my sandwich
and my cup of soup

I Remember

Things I've done
I'll never do again
Things that haunt me
angels and ghosts,
nightmare and reverie

Life lived twice
a thousand times
Thank god
Curse the devil
for the pleasure
and the scourge
of memory

The first touch
of another's lips
The torture
of childish scorn
whispered love
spitting hate
heal me
touch me
more more

I am proud
I am sorry
for what I've done
and I did not do
If only

I say eternally
I could do
it all again
not just in memory

Be Tough
(With apologies to J. Lennon)

Don't give peace a chance
Don't ever
give peace a chance.

Club it.
Smother it.
Kick it in the ass.

All I am saying is
don't give peace a chance.

Knock it to the ground.
Step on it's throat.
Hold it down.

Beat it.
Stab it
'til it
bleeds to death.

Peace is bad for
Business.

Peace doesn't sell no rockets.
Peace don't sell guns.
Peace don't fly no
Aero-planes.

Peace is no damn fun.
Gimme a gun.

Be a badass killer.
Be a thug.

Be tough.
It's the only virtue
we got left.

No faith.
No hope.
No charity.

Love and Kindness?
No siree.

Jesus Christ
couldn't sell
that stuff.
Peace is for pussies.

Don't listen to
that old song.
Johnny Lennon
had it wrong.

Everybody sing.
Everybody dance.
All we are saying is:

Don't
give peace
a fuckin' chance

Love Love

I just love love
some people say
I am in love with "it"
not with her or him,

Well, that may be true
You can be in love that way
Love makes your heart go faster
It takes your breath away

When the phone rings
let it be her
let it be him
you pray

Love makes the day long
and the nights short
the sunsets magical
But I swear to you

I'm not in love
with love that way
I am just in love with you...
and you and you and you

Okay, heavens above,
maybe I am in love with love
infatuated with infatuation
that may indeed be true,

But still, it doesn't mean
I'm not in love with you.

To Hell With Your Soul

You say you like Jesus
You really love rock & roll,
drinkin', druggin' & sex
To hell with your soul

You won't live long with 'em
but can't live without 'em
You're dying to have 'em
if dying you must

You say "pass me the guitar,
the devil may care"
The money you're chasing
says "in God we trust"

Yeah, you may like Jesus
Your true love is rock & roll
That bad life is the good life,
you know what I mean?

When the music stops,
and they turn off the lights
the hang-over starts
you want to come clean

You throw away the bottle
You smash the glass
You pray to Jesus
to save your ass.

But tomorrow night
you'll do it again
You'll pay the toll
because you really do
love to rock and roll

My Lady's Like A Sports Car

Her body's long and lean
her lines are sleek
she's got an engine
that is supercharged
she can really roar
she shifts her gears
she pops her clutch
she spins her wheels
and I scream for more
she hugs the curves
she drifts the turns
she snakes the esses
she burns the straightaway
she sets speed records
she begs me to go slow
she scorns a pit stop
she wins every race
she always ends up on top
My lady's like a sports car
she is hell on wheels

See You Later

When you look,
What do you see?
If you look real hard
you might see me.

When you are young
and looking forward
there is so much
you are dying to see.

When you are old
and close to dying,
don't look back,
you'll see eternity.

I've seen beauty
and I've felt pain.
In your eyes
all I see is mystery.

If I were young
I'd take that challenge,
scale that mountain,
cross that sea.

It's been good
and it's been bad.
I've had the best
a man could have.

Oh my god, I wish
with all my heart,
I could live this
exquisite life again.

Pretty soon
and it won't be long,
you'll look for me
and I'll be gone.

Murder, The Musical

What a world it is
up in here
where boys
gun each other down
in the streets
Girls punch and claw
each other's eyes
Some even carry guns
for the boys
'cause the man cops
can't frisk them
and the artists
glorify it all in music
that drives
the young killers on

It's a wonder
they sing about murder
but they do
as the killers load their guns
it's a mystery
it's crazy why the kids
would ever take a life
for a fucking song
Then they die
and the violence rolls on

You can dance to it
You can rap to it
It makes no sense
but they know
how to wear it
like gold
and make it
all rhyme

Cry Of The Wild

The lions roar
the eagles cry
the bears growl
the elephants trumpet
the gorillas scream
the dogs bark
the wolves howl
the dolphins leap
the wild horses race
the buffalo stampede
the mules kick
the sharks bite
the snakes hiss
the turtles snap
the crows fly

the owls hoot
the hawks dive
the buzzards swoop
the bees swarm
the wind whips
the ocean churns
the fires rage
the ground heaves
the glaciers collapse
the sky weeps
the forest dies

all of nature
pleads please
humans please
save our one
precious Earth
if not for you
then for me.

One And One

Human beings
have two brains
one to think
one to dream
two sets of eyes
one to look ahead
one to look back
two tongues
one to trust
one that lies
two hearts
one to love
one to hate
Human beings
have two lives
or so they say
one is eternal
the other dies

Others

There's a man over there.
Can you see him
playing with his child?
He seems harmless
but look closely.
He doesn't look like you
He's not from here.
His skin is a little off
not the same as yours.
His eyes a different shape,
his lips fuller than yours.
His wife is pushing
the child now on a swing.
Go over there,
take your friends.
Tell them to get out.
Tell then to go home.
If they do not obey,
tell them harder.
If he stands up to you,
knock him down.
Kick him, keep him
on the ground.
Grab his wife,
do what you will with her.
They're all whores,
women not from here.

When the child cries,
slap the kid silly.
His father will attack you.
You can't allow that,
not from someone
who is not from here.
If he keeps fighting,
teach him a lesson,
kill the bastard.
He's not from here.

God Damn It, Please

In the face of a child
is the hope of the world.
But in the blink of an eye
a bomb explodes.
Their bomb, our bomb,
what's the difference?
An end to civility
is the end of the world.

Guilty In Advance

It must be an illness,
some deep affliction
of the heart and soul.
I wake up each day
with shooting pains
and pangs of guilt
for things I've done
but as much for things
that I have not.

Warriors lug PTSD
back from the war.
I've got a dose of
something like that,
but I have never
aimed a goddamned
gun at any one
though I've had one
aimed at me.

I have wounded a few
loved ones and friends.
I know I must suffer
over them forever.
But "guilty-in-advance"
is a judgment that
I really don't deserve.

Someone suggested
it is "original sin"
that is bugging me,
since I was brainwashed
by the priests and nuns
in Catholic School,
and that is a possibility.
My own sins
are not that original
but that original one
must have been a doozy.

Whatever the truth,
I wonder if,
maybe I should just
commit some terrible sin,
some dreadful offense,
utterly unforgiveable,
before I leave the planet.

Since I've got so much
unearned guilt in my
moral bank account,
after I do whatever
awful thing that I may do,

I am just going to
sit back, relax,
with a glass of wine
and some legal weed
that I don't have to
feel guilty about
and be forever satisfied.

Oh, Well, It's Just Hell

Many of my friends are gone now
leaving me behind

As I heedfully look around me
I see that I am next in line

I wonder what will go first
my body or my mind

My looks left me years ago
pretty women trailed them out the door

One perfect lady stood by me
I could not begin to ask for more

Life at the edge of a cliff
tends to keep you on your toes

One false step and you discover
where the road to eternity goes

I am not terribly afraid of dying
and would not admit it if I were

But it's dull to spend forever with God,
It might be more fun with Lucifer

Meanwhile I think I shall pretend
I'm closer the middle than the end

Love Is A Drug

Love is a drug
love is a trip

One little dose
will get you ripped

Don't need pharmaceuticals
to be thrilled to your cuticles

Love is a soporific
It can be an upper or a downer

There's good ones, and bad ones
sometimes all in one

Bummers as low as the ocean floor
highs as high as the bluest sky.

Love is a trip
Love is a drug

You can study it
There's a lot to learn

Accredited or extracurricular
Love's not very particular

It can start with a kiss
or simply a hug

You can do it on a big soft bed
or just do it on the rug

Do it hard as a rock
or limp as a noodle

Keep it simple if you like
or whole kit and caboodle

You can do it with her or him
just don't do it with next of kin.

That's all I can tell you
You must learn for yourself

To do it just a little
go find yourself an elf

John Binder studied literature at Kenyon College. He wrote for the college literary journal, directed theater and acted the lead role in several classic plays there.

He studied acting at H.B. Studios in New York and did graduate work in film at New York University. He formed Paradigm Films with Michael Wadleigh. He worked on two Academy Award Winning Documentaries, "Woodstock", and "Marjoe". He co-produced and edited the award winning anti-war documentary "No Vietnamese Ever Called Me Nigger", which is now in the Smithsonian Museum film collection. He co-directed "Four Children", winner of the White House Film prize for government-funded documentaries.

In Hollywood, he worked for Robert Altman. He wrote "Endangered Species" for Alan Rudolph, and "Honeysuckle Rose" for producer Sidney Pollack. He won the American Heritage award for scripting a CBS movie "Sam Houston. He wrote and directed the feature film "UFOria" with Fred Ward, Cindy Williams, and Harry Dean Stanton. "UFOria" made the top ten film lists (1986) of The New York Times, The Los Angeles Times, The Boston Globe, The Chicago Tribune, LA Weekly and others. He wrote and co-directed a full-length play "Dreams Die Hard". He wrote and directed three short films, New Listing, Where's My Sandwich", and "Fatal Femme". This is his second book of poetry. He's published two novellas as well.

He lives in Los Angeles with his wife Jeanne Field. Sons, Josh and John Henry and their families live near by.